The Literature of Cinema

ADVISORY EDITOR: **MARTIN S. DWORKIN**
INSTITUTE OF PHILOSOPHY AND POLITICS OF EDUCATION
TEACHER'S COLLEGE, COLUMBIA UNIVERSITY

THE LITERATURE OF CINEMA presents a comprehensive selection from the multitude of writings about cinema, rediscovering materials on its origins, history, theoretical principles and techniques, aesthetics, economics, and effects on societies and individuals. Included are works of inherent, lasting merit and others of primarily historical significance. These provide essential resources for serious study and critical enjoyment of the "magic shadows" that became one of the decisive cultural forces of modern times.

Motion Pictures and Youth

A Summary

W. W. Charters

ARNO PRESS & THE NEW YORK TIMES

New York • 1970

Reprint Edition 1970 by Arno Press Inc.
Library of Congress Catalog Card Number: 73-124025
ISBN 0-405-01642-5
ISBN for complete set: 0-405-01600-X
Manufactured in the United States of America

MOTION PICTURES AND YOUTH: A SUMMARY

———

MOTION PICTURES AND YOUTH

THE PAYNE FUND STUDIES

W. W. CHARTERS, CHAIRMAN

MOTION PICTURES AND YOUTH: A SUMMARY, by W. W. Charters, Director, Bureau of Educational Research, Ohio State University.

Combined with

GETTING IDEAS FROM THE MOVIES, by P. W. Holaday, Indianapolis Public Schools, and George D. Stoddard, Director, Iowa Child Welfare Research Station.

MOTION PICTURES AND THE SOCIAL ATTITUDES OF CHILDREN, by Ruth C. Peterson and L. L. Thurstone, Department of Psychology, University of Chicago.

Combined with

THE SOCIAL CONDUCT AND ATTITUDES OF MOVIE FANS, by Frank K. Shuttleworth and Mark A. May, Institute of Human Relations, Yale University.

THE EMOTIONAL RESPONSES OF CHILDREN TO THE MOTION PICTURE SITUATION, by W. S. Dysinger and Christian A. Ruckmick, Department of Psychology, State University of Iowa.

Combined with

MOTION PICTURES AND STANDARDS OF MORALITY, by Charles C. Peters, Professor of Education, Pennsylvania State College.

CHILDREN'S SLEEP, by Samuel Renshaw, Vernon L. Miller, and Dorothy Marquis, Department of Psychology, Ohio State University.

MOVIES AND CONDUCT, by Herbert Blumer, Department of Sociology, University of Chicago.

THE CONTENT OF MOTION PICTURES, by Edgar Dale, Research Associate, Bureau of Educational Research, Ohio State University.

Combined with

CHILDREN'S ATTENDANCE AT MOTION PICTURES, by Edgar Dale.

MOVIES, DELINQUENCY, AND CRIME, by Herbert Blumer and Philip M. Hauser, Department of Sociology, University of Chicago.

BOYS, MOVIES, AND CITY STREETS, by Paul G. Cressey and Frederick M. Thrasher, New York University.

HOW TO APPRECIATE MOTION PICTURES, by Edgar Dale, Research Associate, Bureau of Educational Research, Ohio State University.

MOTION PICTURES AND YOUTH

A SUMMARY

❖

W. W. CHARTERS
DIRECTOR, BUREAU OF EDUCATIONAL RESEARCH,
OHIO STATE UNIVERSITY

NEW YORK
THE MACMILLAN COMPANY
1933

THIS SERIES OF TWELVE STUDIES OF THE
INFLUENCE OF MOTION PICTURES UPON
CHILDREN AND YOUTH HAS BEEN MADE BY
THE COMMITTEE ON EDUCATIONAL RE-
SEARCH OF THE PAYNE FUND AT THE RE-
QUEST OF THE NATIONAL COMMITTEE FOR
THE STUDY OF SOCIAL VALUES IN MOTION
PICTURES, NOW THE MOTION PICTURE RE-
SEARCH COUNCIL, 366 MADISON AVENUE,
NEW YORK CITY. THE STUDIES WERE DE-
SIGNED TO SECURE AUTHORITATIVE AND
IMPERSONAL DATA WHICH WOULD MAKE
POSSIBLE A MORE COMPLETE EVALUATION
OF MOTION PICTURES AND THEIR SOCIAL
POTENTIALITIES

CHAIRMAN'S PREFACE

MOTION PICTURES are not understood by the present generation of adults. They are new; they make an enormous appeal to children; and they present ideas and situations which parents may not like. Consequently when parents think of the welfare of their children who are exposed to these compelling situations, they wonder about the effect of the pictures upon the ideals and behavior of the children. Do the pictures really influence children in any direction? Are their conduct, ideals, and attitudes affected by the movies? Are the scenes which are objectionable to adults understood by children, or at least by very young children? Do children eventually become sophisticated and grow superior to pictures? Are the emotions of children harmfully excited? In short, just what effect do motion pictures have upon children of different ages?

Each individual has his answer to these questions. He knows of this or that incident in his own experience, and upon these he bases his conclusions. Consequently opinions differ widely. No one in this country up to the present time has known in any general and impersonal manner just what effect motion pictures have upon children. Meanwhile children clamor to attend the movies as often as they are allowed to go. Moving pictures make a profound appeal to children of all ages. In such a situation it is obvious that a comprehensive study of the influence of motion pictures upon children and youth is appropriate.

To measure these influences the investigators who co-operated to make this series of studies analyzed the problem to discover the most significant questions involved. They set up individual studies to ascertain the answer to the questions and to provide a composite answer to the central question of the nature and extent of these influences. In using this technique the answers must inevitably be sketches without all the details filled in; but when the details are added the picture will not be changed in any essential manner. Parents, educators, and physicians will have little difficulty in fitting concrete details of their own into the outlines which these studies supply.

Specifically, the studies were designed to form a series to answer the following questions: What sorts of scenes do the children of America see when they attend the theaters? How do the mores depicted in these scenes compare with those of the community? How often do children attend? How much of what they see do they remember? What effect does what they witness have upon their ideals and attitudes? Upon their sleep and health? Upon their emotions? Do motion pictures directly or indirectly affect the conduct of children? Are they related to delinquency and crime, and, finally, how can we teach children to discriminate between movies that are artistically and morally good and bad?

The history of the investigations is brief. In 1928 William H. Short, Executive Director of the Motion Picture Research Council, invited a group of university psychologists, sociologists, and educators to meet with the members of the Council to confer about the possibility of discovering just what effect motion pictures have upon children, a subject, as has been indicated, upon which many conflicting opinions and few substantial facts were in existence. The university men proposed a program of study. When Mr. Short appealed to The Payne Fund for a grant to support such an investigation, he found the foundation receptive because of its well-known interest in motion pictures as one of the major influences in the lives of modern youth. When the appropriation had been made the investigators organized themselves into a Committee on Educational Research of The Payne Fund with the following membership: L. L. Thurstone, Frank N. Freeman, R. E. Park, Herbert Blumer, Philip M. Hauser of the University of Chicago; George D. Stoddard, Christian A. Ruckmick, P. W. Holaday, and Wendell Dysinger of the University of Iowa; Mark A. May and Frank K. Shuttleworth of Yale University; Frederick M. Thrasher and Paul G. Cressey of New York University; Charles C. Peters of Pennsylvania State College; Ben D. Wood of Columbia University; and Samuel Renshaw, Edgar Dale, and W. W. Charters of Ohio State University. The investigations have extended through four years, 1929–1932, inclusive.

The committee's work is an illustration of an interesting technique for studying any social problem. The distinctive characteristic of this technique is to analyze a complex social problem into a series of subordinate problems, to select competent investigators to work upon each of the subordinate projects and to integrate the findings of all the investigators as a solution of the initial problem. Such a program yields a skeleton framework, which, while somewhat lacking in detail, is substantially correct if the contributing investigations have been validly conducted. To provide this framework or outline is the task of research. To fill in the detail and to provide the interpretations are the natural and easy tasks of those who use the data.

W. W. C.

Ohio State University
September, 1933

MOTION PICTURES AND YOUTH

THE INITIATION OF THE STUDIES

AT the initial meeting of the investigators with the Motion Picture Research Council they found that the Council had a comprehensive group of problems upon which they were seeking data for the development of a national policy concerning motion pictures. Later these were formulated as a series of two score questions relating to the effect of motion pictures upon children, youth, adults, and communities; the effect of current motion pictures upon the impressions that foreign countries gain of the United States; how well the motion-picture industry is organized to perform its social responsibilities; what may be accomplished through governmental agencies to control the effects of the motion pictures; and how a campaign of education may be organized to produce socially desirable results.

The investigators first proceeded to eliminate certain areas of study indicated in the questions with which they were not competent to deal. Specifically they were not equipped to discover what attitudes toward American life current motion pictures were creating abroad. While this problem would easily yield to investigation it involved a separate organization and a substantial subsidy. A study of the financial, legal, economic, and administrative virtues and vices of the motion-picture industry was not undertaken because this problem belonged primarily in the field of economics and business while our group of investigators

1

were psychologists, sociologists, and educators. Nor did the group investigate and assemble methods of educating the public with regard to the control of motion pictures beyond the preparation of materials on motion-picture appreciation and criticism for the use of high-school students. These studies will be undertaken for the Motion Picture Research Council by competent investigators when the depression lifts.

The investigators did feel, however, that they would enjoy the opportunity to assemble data in answer to a number of the other questions proposed.

The Council asked, "What is the amount of knowledge gained and retained from motion pictures by children of various ages and the types of the knowledge most likely to be thus gained and retained?" Holaday and Stoddard have answered the first half of the question quite adequately and with four others of the group have indicated an answer to the second half.

The Council also wanted to know "the extent to which motion pictures influence the conduct of children and youth either in desirable or undesirable directions and particularly in regard to patterns of sex behavior." Blumer in his conduct study, Blumer and Hauser in their delinquency study, and Cressey and Thrasher have assembled massive and significant data upon this question.

What effect motion pictures have upon the attitudes of children toward significant social concepts, standards, and ideals of children was a matter of concern to the Council. Upon this point data have been assembled by Peterson and Thurstone and by May and Shuttleworth.

We were asked to discover the effect of motion pictures upon the health of children. While no direct attack was made upon the problem an interesting indirect attack was developed by Renshaw, Miller, and Marquis, in the study of the influence of motion-picture attendance upon restlessness in sleep which is in turn related to the health of children. The Council also wished to know whether or not motion pictures influenced the emotions of children and whether this influence if established was exerted in wholesome or in harmful ways. Upon the first half of this problem a study was made by Dysinger and Ruckmick; on the second half data were assembled by Blumer and Hauser and by Cressey and Thrasher.

The Council raised a number of questions concerning the effect of current commercial films upon the standards of American life. It wanted to know "the characteristics of good motion pictures in the opinion of different intelligence levels and social groups" and was concerned about the respects in which current pictures shown in commercial theaters measured up to or offended against these standards. These question were studied directly by Peters, who developed techniques for the investigation of the problem and used them on four types of content.

Of major interest to the Council was an analysis of the content of current films. It felt that if it were proved that children acquired information, changed attitudes, and modified conduct as a result of movie attendance the directions in which these changes occurred would be determined by what they saw in the movies. Dale analyzed the content of several hundred films and classified the types of scenes which were presented.

The Council wished also to know the number of children by ages who attended motion-picture theaters and the frequency with which they made their visits. This information was collected by Dale.

Finally the Council was interested in knowing what could

be done to teach children to discriminate between good and poor movies. In studying this problem Dale produced a textbook on motion-picture appreciation for high-school children.

Some questions in this area were not answered. We did not rank the motion pictures in a scale of influence in relation to other agencies such as the home, the school, the church, and the press. To rank these factors according to greater or less influence with objective accuracy is impossible with any known techniques. It is apparent in the interpretations of Blumer, Thrasher, May, and others that many agencies exert an influence upon children and that of these the movies are one.

The investigators sought to find data, but could not, to prove that the onset of puberty is or is not affected by motion pictures. (The age of the onset of puberty had not been fixed in scientific studies prior to the advent of the movies.) They were asked to find out whether or not motion pictures stifled the imagination of children, healthfully stimulated it, over-stimulated its action, or whether their effects were greater or less than that of books. These questions we did not investigate. Although the Council wished to know whether or not our findings for children were valid for adults we confined our attention for the most part to children and youth and used adults only occasionally for comparison in specific cases.

Summarizing, we may say that instead of attacking individually each of a score or more of the questions proposed, the investigators set up a few basic studies which when completed would provide data for answering completely or in part a wide range of separate queries.

THE PLAN OF THE STUDIES

THE studies fall naturally into two groups: one, to measure the effect of motion pictures as such upon children and youth; the other, to study current motion-picture content and children's attendance at commercial movie theaters to see what they come in contact with when they attend them.

In measuring the effect of pictures upon children the studies were focused on influences upon behavior and conduct. Proceeding from this objective by analysis it was logical to set up studies of information, attitudes, health, and emotions as well as upon one-to-one correspondence between motion pictures and child behavior. This is a logical procedure because behavior may safely be assumed to be influenced by what one knows, by his attitudes, by his emotions, and by the condition of his health.

Then on the basis of what is discovered to be the effect of motion pictures upon these five areas—information, attitudes, emotions, health, and conduct—it is possible to gauge the effect of current commercial motion pictures upon children by ascertaining two facts: what they see when they attend the theaters and how often they go. If, in short, the general influence of motion pictures is ascertained, if the content is known and the number of visits of children has been computed, the total influence of the pictures will be in general a product of these three factors. That is to say, if motion pictures have any influence upon children, if the pictures are good and if the attendance is optimally spaced we can assume that the influence upon behavior will be beneficial. If motion pictures have no influence it will not matter from that point of view whether children go to the movies or not nor what they see when they go. If, however, an influence is discovered, if the pictures are bad, and if children attend the theater we may reasonably assume that the influence upon conduct will be harmful.

The major interest of the investigators was directed to the measurement of influence because it is important to know that pictures do or do not exhibit potency without respect to goodness or badness. If it is established that children are moved by pictures toward dislike for one social value and toward liking for another, and if it is shown that both facts and errors are learned and remembered, it is apparent that motion pictures have fundamental influences which may be exerted in any direction. The range and limits of the potency of motion pictures are of major significance to educators and are fundamental to the drawing of inferences in a very large number of areas.

The interest of the investigators in the content of the current motion-picture situation was minor in the sense that if movies should permanently exert a strong influence upon a variety of social standards and activities the current pictures can be changed in tone and attitude with much greater ease in the long view than can the psychological and educational effects of pictures as such. If the influence of the motion picture can be measured, validated, and interpreted with accuracy the formulas so obtained can be applied to all pictures to discover with validity whether they are having beneficial or harmful effects upon children. They become measuring instruments to apply to the movies which are now being exhibited or with equal propriety to the pictures which will supplant the current films.

Yet while some investigators were primarily interested in establishing measuring instruments because of their usefulness as measures to be used on all kinds of pictures, others were concerned about the effect of the current run of pictures in the commercial theater upon the present generation of children and youth. And by combining the factors studied we are able to provide an indication of the influence of current commercial films upon the behavior of individuals and the standards of communities.

Finally, the group worked as individuals to provide answers to specific fundamental questions. They did not attempt to draw general conclusions from all the studies. The chairman, however, was given the commission of making the following interpretation of the findings for the consideration of the Motion Picture Research Council and the information of the public.

LEARNING FACTS

How much information children acquire from the movies is a question of interest to parents and is a matter of concern to them when their children view pictures which the parents do not like. In the latter case, the problem is accompanied by fear if the parent believes that his children learn much from the picture and is dismissed lightly if he thinks that most of what they see passes over their heads.

To the question of how much children retain of what is in a picture for them to see, Holaday and Stoddard directed their attention in a three-year study.[1] They used seventeen commercial pictures such as "Tom Sawyer," "New Moon," "Stolen Heaven," "Rango," "Passion Flower," and "Fighting Caravans." Somewhat over 3,000 children and adults participated in the study as observers. They were selected in four age groups which were all given the same tests upon the information acquired. These tests were of two types, one testing the retention of the plot of the story—the actions and sayings of the actors,—the other testing the general information of historical, geographical, or mechanical items. To the 3,000 individuals were administered a total of 26 tests each containing from 30 to 64 factual items and producing an aggregate of more than 20,000 testings for a total of 813,000 items attempted. Proper precautions were

[1] *Getting Ideas fro m the Movies*, by P. W. Holaday and George D. Stoddard.

taken to equate groups for age, intelligence, and the like so that the results from group to group might be comparable. Careful statistical techniques were utilized. The most striking conclusion translated roughly into concrete language is this. If parents take their 8 year old child to the movies he will catch three out of every five items that the parents catch. This conclusion is arrived at somewhat as follows. The next day after viewing each of six pictures in 1930 to 1931 and answering a total of approximately 400 carefully selected questions dealing with items appearing in the scenes, 162 "superior" adults—young college professors, graduate students and their wives —made a score of 87.8 out of a possible 100. At the same time 959 children in grades 2 and 3 made a score of 52.5. Coincidentally 1,180 children in grades 5 and 6 made a score of 65.9 and youths in grades 9 and 10 achieved a score of 80.9. Thus using the adult score as a basis, children of 8 and 9 years made 60 per cent, those of 11 and 12 made 75 per cent, and children of 15 and 16 made 91 per cent of the score obtained by adults. Hence roughly speaking a parent who is a superior adult can count upon his young child to see approximately 3 out of the 5 things he sees, his 11 or 12 year old child to see 3 out of 4, and his 15 or 16 year old to catch 9 out of 10. Or putting the conclusion in another way the 8 or 9 year old sees half of what is to be seen, the 11 or 12 year old two thirds, and the 15 or 16 year old four fifths of what is to be seen. This is true if we assume, as a reading of the study demonstrates, that the questions in the tests are a reasonably fair sample of the questions that might be asked. The amount of information acquired is very high.

A second interesting fact relates to the surprising amount the children remember about a picture six weeks and three months later. In general the second-third-grade children at the end of six weeks remember 90 per cent of what they knew on the day following the show. Three months after seeing the picture they remember as much as they did six weeks after seeing it. In some cases, as with ".Tom Sawyer," they remember more at the end of six weeks and still more at the end of three months. At all ages including the adults the slow drop of the curve of forgetting is striking. The investigators conclude from the data that the "curves of retention are considerably higher than those obtained by previous investigators (using other materials) and motion pictures appear to make a greater contribution to visual education than was previously suspected." [2]

Of interest is an implication lying within the fact that very young children remember correctly 50 or 60 per cent of what they see. Conversely this means that they do not get 50 or 40 per cent of what they see. When they do not answer questions accurately it may not mean that their memories are blank on those points. They may have acquired misinformation. Dysinger and Ruckmick found in their interviews that children frequently misunderstood the meaning of what they had seen and thereby reacted in unexpected fashion at their "reading points."

A third interesting fact of educational significance drawn from the study is this. Children of all ages tend to accept as authentic what they see in the movies. Thus pre-tests on general information were given to groups and their scores were computed. Then equated groups viewed pictures in which were shown the errors of fact which had been covered in the pre-tests. The two sets of scores were compared and it was found that at each of the three age levels the incorrectly shown items had left their marks. The children had

[2] When quotation marks are used they inclose the statements of the investigators.

increased their fund of knowledge on the correctly shown items covered by the test, but their acceptance of the incorrect items as correct had lowered their improvement in their total scores. They tended to accept the errors as facts. In general "children accept the information in the movies as correct unless it is flagrantly incorrect." It is of interest to know the types of fact that children remember best. The investigators divided the facts into ten classes and found that "action was remembered best when it concerned sports, general conversation, crime, and fighting, when it had a high emotional tonus and when it occurred in a familiar type of surrounding such as home, school, or tenement. . . . It was understood least when it concerned unfamiliar activities such as bootlegging and business, when it had practically no emotional tonus, and when it occurred in surroundings of an unfamiliar and interesting type such as café and frontier."

The types of information tested in this study are supplemented by the Blumer and Thrasher [3] studies. They analyze the rôle of the movies as a source of information which is noticed and copied by adolescents. In their studies they mass cases covering a wide variety of areas in which information is acquired and used: hints on how to beautify one's self and wear one's clothes, examples of attractive mannerisms, and demonstrations of satisfying love techniques. To these they add patterns for the play of children, suggestions for delinquent action and crime upon occasion. None of these was measured by Blumer and Thrasher with the Holaday-Stoddard techniques, but it may reasonably be assumed that the acquisition of facts in these specific areas described by Blumer and Thrasher proceeds with the

[3] *Movies and Conduct*, by Herbert Blumer: *Motion Pictures, Delinquency, and Crime*, by Herbert Blumer and Philip M. Hauser; *Boys, Movies, and City Streets*, by Paul G. Cressey and Frederick M. Thrasher.

same effectiveness as in the areas studied by Holaday and Stoddard.

Finally no significant sex differences appeared in the amount of information acquired or the amount remembered at later dates. Girls and boys remember about equally well. In summary Holaday and Stoddard have shown that the amount of information gained from motion pictures by children of all ages including the 8 and 9 year olds is "tremendously high." This constitutes the first link in the sequential chain of the inquiry into the influence of motion pictures upon children and youth.

Developing Attitudes

Because a close relationship between the attitude of an individual and his actions may be assumed, the study of the effect of motion pictures upon the attitude of children toward important social values is central in importance. The investigations of May and Shuttleworth and of Peterson and Thurstone are consequently interesting links in the chain of studies. May and Shuttleworth [4] conducted two studies: one on the correlation between movie attendance and character and another on the relation of attendance to attitudes toward objects of social interest.

In the first study they selected in three communities 102 children who attended the movies from four to five times a week and 101 other children who attended about twice a month. Each group was about equally divided between boys and girls. The groups were equated for age, sex, school grade, intelligence, occupational level of the father, and cultural home background.

The "movie" and "non-movie" children were compared as to reputation in school among teachers and classmates.

[4] *The Social Conduct and Attitudes of Movie Fans*, by Frank K. Shuttleworth and Mark A. May.

Reputation was measured by six factors: deportment; scholastic work; a conduct record (consisting of tests on coöperation, reliability, persistence, and the like); a check list of descriptive adjectives marked by teachers; a "Guess Who" instrument in which children told who among their classmates met certain specified qualifications; and a "Best Friend" device by which children indicated those among their classmates who were their best friends.

The investigators report: "We have found that the movie children average lower deportment records, do on the average poorer work in their school subjects, are rated lower in reputation by teachers on two rating forms, are rated lower by their classmates on the 'Guess Who' test, are less coöperative and less controlled as measured both by ratings and conduct tests, are slightly more deceptive in school situations, are slightly less skillful in judging what is the most useful and helpful and sensible thing to do, and are slightly less emotionally stable. Against this long record, the movie children are superior on only two measures: They are mentioned more frequently on the 'Guess Who' test as a whole and are named more frequently as best friends by their classmates. Tests showing no differences also need cataloging. These include honesty rating and honesty as measured in out-of-school situations, persistence, suggestibility, and moral knowledge."

Cressey and Thrasher [5] in their study of a congested area in New York City found conditions of similar import. Of 949 boys studied in the area about one quarter were retarded and another quarter were accelerated in school. Of those who attended the movies 4 times a week or more 19 per cent were accelerated in school, 24 per cent were normal, and 57 per cent were retarded. Of those, however,

[5] *Boys, Movies, and City Streets*, by Paul G. Cressey and Frederick M. Thrasher.

who attended once a week or less 35 per cent were accelerated, 33 per cent were normal, and 32 per cent were retarded. The movie group contained nearly twice as many retarded pupils and half as many accelerated pupils as the non-movie children.

Cressey and Thrasher also discovered in this area that among 1,356 boys 109 were delinquents. Of these 22 per cent attended the movies 3 times or more a week and 6 per cent attended less than once a week, while among those who were not delinquent 14 per cent attended 3 times or more a week and 6 per cent attended less than once a week. These figures indicate that for this population there is a positive relationship between truancy and delinquency and frequent movie attendance.

An important question arises at this point. Does extreme movie attendance lead to conduct which harms reputation or do children of low reputation go frequently to the movies? It rises also at other points. Thrasher and Blumer and their associates as they present their cases are faced by the same question and discuss it. The authors who raise the question express the general conclusion that a simple cause and effect relationship does not prevail. To say that the movies are solely responsible for anti-social conduct, delinquency, or crime is not valid. To assert contrariwise that delinquents and criminals happen to frequent the movies and are not affected by them is clearly indefensible. Validity probably rests with a combination of the two—tendencies toward unapproved conduct and movie influence work together to produce more movie interest on the one hand and more anti-social conduct on the other. The two factors drive toward progressive aggravation of unhealthful conditions.

Turning from their conduct study to their attitudes

study, we find that May and Shuttleworth searched diligently for specific criticisms of the movies in literature, in conversation, and the like, and divided them into twelve classes: heroes and boobs of the movies, the people of other lands, prohibition, crime and criminals, sex attitudes, attitude toward schools, clothing, militarism, personal attitude, escape from threatening danger, special dislikes, and a miscellaneous group. For each of the first eleven classes an hypothesis was advanced concerning the effect of the movies upon that particular area. The responsibility of the investigators was to find out whether or not this hypothesis was true. For instance, for the class, heroes and boobs of the movies, the investigators selected the hypothesis that there is a tendency for the movies to place certain characters in a favorable light and to hold up others to ridicule. Their task was to discover whether or not this hypothesis was correct; that is, whether movie and non-movie children showed significant differences in their attitudes toward characters shown in the movies, athletes, Protestant ministers, actors, cowboys, college professors, policemen, and the like.

To explore the eleven hypotheses of which the foregoing is an illustration approximately 250 questions were prepared, making an average of about 22 questions in each area. They thus covered by this procedure all the statements that they could discover about the influence of the movies upon attitudes.

The investigators then selected from large populations of children groups which attended the movies frequently and others which attended them infrequently. The movie groups attended the theater nearly three times a week while the non-movie groups attended less than once a month. Unfortunately, enough children could not be found for their uses who had never attended the movies. The investigators were compelled, therefore, to use children in the groups who had gone to the movies twice a month or less. But the movie group had attended twelve times as often as the other group. Four hundred sixteen movie cases and 443 non-movie cases were studied. These groups were equated for age, school grade, intelligence, socio-economic-educational background, and a few other special factors in individual localities. Equal proportions of boys and girls were included. To each of the groups, movie and non-movie, were given series of statements upon which it was thought there might be discernible differences which might possibly be attributed to movie attendance. These statements occurred usually in the form: "All Most Many Some Few No Chinese are cunning and underhand." Each child was then required to underline one word which best expressed his attitude toward the Chinese. Questions were also used such as, "Which would you rather be, a college professor or a cowboy?" Some true-false statements were included, as "Most Russians are kind and generous." The replies were then tabulated for the movie and the non-movie groups and the differences were observed to see whether or not they were statistically significant.

On the basis of the questions and statements used, no significant differences in attitude were discovered between the movie and non-movie groups on a number of objects including athletics, the Chinese, robbers, gang leaders, rum runners, prohibition agents, prohibition enforcement, the success of marriage, sex attitudes, and the like. Significant differences were found in that movie children admire cowboys, popular actors, dancers, and chorus girls while non-movie children are more interested in such types as the medical student and the college professor. Movie children are more inclined to believe that much drinking and violation of the prohibition laws exist. Movie children set special value on smart clothes and dressing well. They are also more sensitive about parental control. The movie children go to more dances and read more; but the quality of their reading is not high.

They say in conclusion: "That the movies exert an influence there can be no doubt. But it is our opinion that this influence is specific for a given child and a given movie. The same picture may influence different children in distinctly opposite directions. Thus in a general survey such as we have made, the net effect appears small. We are also convinced that among the most frequent attendants the movies are drawing children who are in some way maladjusted and whose difficulties are relieved only in the most temporary manner and are, in fact, much aggravated. In other words, the movies tend to fix and further establish the behavior patterns and types of attitudes which already exist among those who attend most frequently."

This attitude study of May and Shuttleworth is of peculiar interest because it is the only one in which the influence of the motion picture is not clearly apparent either as cause or effect or as an aggravation of precedent conditions. Superficially one might claim that this study indicates that motion pictures have no influence upon boys and girls. That position May and Shuttleworth do not take. They say that movies do exert an influence upon children and indicate that this influence is greater than appears on the surface. The studies of Stoddard, Thurstone, Blumer, Thrasher, and their associates support this position with a huge mass of specific data.

The causes of this neutral effect are several. May says "We were conducting a survey and not an experiment;

we were not attempting to measure attitudes precisely but rather to sample them widely; we recognized that specific undesirable effects may be cancelled by specific desirable effects and that the desirable net effects may be cancelled by some other agency." They advance the theory also that the influence of motion pictures "is specific for a given movie." This is supported by Renshaw, Ruckmick, and other investigators. Other factors operate to produce neutrality.

The measuring instrument of attitudes used in their survey was not so sensitive as that of Peterson and Thurstone which showed positive effects with specific pictures. Peterson-Thurstone scales utilized 25 to 30 units integrated into a total product; the May-Shuttleworth techniques used single units which were considered as disparate items and were not integrated into a single scale of attitudes. The relative results of the survey techniques of May and Shuttleworth and of the experimental techniques of Peterson and Thurstone are roughly analogous to the determination of bodily temperature by the hand and by a thermometer. Fine significant differences which may be read on the thermometer may not be perceived by the hand.

The May-Shuttleworth study is of chief value as a caution. It indicates clearly that the influence of a motion picture is only one of several influences and the attitudes of children are a product of many influences. Native temperament, past experience, family ideals, school instruction, community mores, all theoretically have an effect. The movies themselves conflict with one another in the direction of their influence—a good picture may be followed by a bad, an anti-Chinese film may be neutralized by a pro-Chinese movie. Results may be produced by the influences of other factors. The home influence may be stronger than the movie in specific cases. School instruction may neutralize the influence of a picture. Sometimes the movie may crash through and overpower the influence of the home, the school, or the community. The total effect of all these influences on the child is analogous to the total effect of an orchestra upon an audience. The violins, the flutes, the brasses contribute to the total orchestral effect. Which instrument is of most importance in the orchestra is an academic question. But a lover of music is much concerned about any one of the instruments which produces sour notes. He demands a workmanlike contribution from every player. So with the movies, the lover of children is concerned with the question of how well the commercial motion picture plays its individual part in the education of children and not with whether it is more or less important than another instrument.

Peterson and Thurstone by the use of different techniques isolated the influence of specific pictures upon groups of children while keeping constant the factors of community standards, habits of children, school influence, home training, and the like. They assumed that these had not materially influenced the children in the brief period between their first and second tests of attitudes; the factor that had changed during the period was exposure to a specific film.

These investigators used eleven highly sensitive instruments to discover changes in attitude toward or against the following eight social objects: the Germans (a scale and a paired comparison), war, (two scales) crime, prohibition, the Chinese, capital punishment, the punishment of criminals (two scales), and the Negro. The instruments were scales which consisted of approximately thirty statements each expressing an attitude toward an object. These statements varied in intensity of position from one extreme of attitude against the object to the other extreme of attitude in favor of the object. The statements were weighted according to techniques described in the study [6] and a total score was computed for each individual to express his attitude toward an object.

The scales were given to high-school children shortly before a picture was seen and the position of the group upon the scale was computed. The picture (which in all cases the children had not seen before) was shown and approximately the day after the showing the scale was given again. The new position of the groups was computed and the resulting change in position noted. In some cases the scale was again checked by some of the groups after two and one-half, five, eight, and nineteen months had elapsed to determine the permanence of the changes which were noted the day after the showing of the picture.

Approximately 4,000 individuals participated in the study as subjects. Most of the subjects were junior and senior high-school students. The exceptions were three in number. In one study 246 college students were used and in another about 100 fourth- and fifth-grade children checked the scale while in three other studies sixth-grade children were included with the junior and senior high-school students. The children were located in the schools of small towns in the neighborhood of Chicago and at Mooseheart, the children's home supported by the Loyal Order of Moose. Small towns were chosen primarily because of the ease of selecting pictures which had not been seen by the children.

Thirteen pictures were selected which met three criteria: they definitely pertained to the issues to be studied, they

[6] *Motion Pictures and the Social Attitudes of Children*, by Ruth C. Peterson and L. L. Thurstone.

were free enough from objectionable matter so that high-school principals could be asked to send their students to see them, and they were sufficiently recent to eliminate distractions caused by fashions or photography. Between 600 and 800 pictures of all kinds were reviewed and from them the thirteen used in the studies were selected. This selection represents an attempt to secure films which would in the judgment of the reviewers be likely to produce a noticeable change in attitude if changes were produced by any pictures. All, however, were well-known films. The titles and issues were: "Four Sons" (on the Germans and war); "Street of Chance" (gambling); "Hide Out" (prohibition); "Son of the Gods" (the Chinese); "Welcome Danger" (the Chinese); "The Valiant" (capital punishment); "Journey's End" (war); "All Quiet on the Western Front" (war); "The Criminal Code" (punishment of criminals); "Alibi" (punishment of criminals); "The Birth of a Nation" (the Negro); "Big House" (punishment of criminals); and "Numbered Men" (punishment of criminals).

The outstanding contribution of the study is the establishment of the fact that the attitude of children toward a social value can be measurably changed by one exposure to a picture. An outstanding picture of potency in its influence upon attitude was "Son of the Gods," a picture selected because it was thought to be favorable to the Chinese. Prior to the showing of the picture the mean attitude of a population of 182 children from grades 9 to 12 inclusive stood at 6.72 on a scale in which the extreme positions were approximately 3.5 at the favorable end of the scale and 9.5 at the unfavorable end. After the children had seen the picture the mean shifted 1.22 steps in a favorable direction from 6.72 to 5.50 and this difference was 17.5 times the probable error of the differences. The shift in attitude is "very striking." "The Birth of a Nation" was shown to 434 children of grades 6 to 12 inclusive. Prior to the showing the mean position of this population was 7.41 with extremes of approximately 2.5 at the unfavorable end of the scale to approximately 9.5 at the favorable end. After exposure to the picture the position shifted in an unfavorable direction to 5.93 with a difference of 1.48, which was 25.5 times the probable error of the differences. This was the largest shift obtained in the studies. "All Quiet on the Western Front" produced in 214 junior and senior high-school students a shift against war 14.98 times the probable error of the differences and "The Criminal Code" a shift against the punishment of criminals 12.2 times the probable error of the difference with 246 college students and 11.7 times against the same issue with 276 high-school students. These were the outstanding cases. Significant results were obtained, also, from the showing of "Four Sons" upon attitude toward the Germans, "Welcome Danger," "The Valiant," and "All Quiet on the Western Front." Statistically important changes did not result from single showings of "Four Sons" upon the attitude toward war, of "Hide Out" toward prohibition, of "Journey's End," with one group, toward war, and "Alibi," "Big House," and "Numbered Men" toward the punishment of criminals. In all of these cases but one the differences, however, were in the expected direction. In "Street of Chance" the investigators expected to discover a change of attitude favorable to gambling but a significant change against gambling was recorded.

The range of influence of the motion picture is sensibly broadened by a second fact which these attitude studies have discovered. The investigators found that the effect of pictures upon attitude is cumulative. They demonstrated the fact that two pictures are more powerful than one and three are more potent than two. At Mooseheart, when "Big House" was shown to 138 junior and senior high-school children and "Numbered Men" to another group of 168, neither produced a statistically significant shift in attitude toward the punishment of criminals. When both pictures were seen by a group the change became significant. The shift was then 3.0 times the probable error of the differences. When to these two exposures was added exposure to a third film on the same subject, "The Criminal Code," the shift was still greater and amounted to 6.7 times the probable error.

Again at Mooseheart "Journey's End" and "All Quiet on the Western Front" were shown separately and in combination. These pictures had individual potency. "Journey's End" alone caused a shift of 5.07 times the probable error against war and "All Quiet on the Western Front" produced one of 6.07 times in the same direction. When the former was followed by the latter the shift was increased to 8.07 times the probable error and when the latter was followed by the former the amount of change was increased to 8.26 times.

This pair of studies indicates a significant hypothesis, namely, that even though one picture related to a social issue may not significantly affect the attitude of an individual or a group, continued exposure to pictures of similar character will in the end produce a measurable change of attitude. What the range and limits of such influence may be we do not know. Whether or not it is true in this area that the repetitions of exposure would increase indefinitely is a subject worthy of investigation. Whether or not there is a threshold of personal sensitivity in children above which many pictures do not rise in power and influence we cannot say. But it is worth while to know that under the conditions of these studies at least, the cumulative effect of pictures upon attitudes is unmistakably indicated.

To these two leads into the influence of motion pictures upon attitudes Peterson and Thurstone have added a third. They have shown that the shifts created by exposure to a film have substantial permanence. In six localities the attitude scales were repeated at varying intervals and changes in average positions of the groups were computed. The case of the high school at Geneva, Illinois, is typical. Before seeing the film, "Son of the Gods," the children's position on a scale of attitude toward the Chinese was 6.61 and promptly after seeing the film it was 5.19—a shift in favor of the Chinese. Five months after seeing the film there was a recession to 5.72 toward the original position of 5.19 and nineteen months later the position was 5.76. That is to say, the effect of the film had not worn off in a year and a half. In none of the six localities was the recession complete except in one. At Paxton, Illinois, the original position was 4.34 on the scale of attitude toward war before exposure to the film, "All Quiet on the Western Front." After viewing the picture the group shifted to 3.74, indicating a less favorable attitude toward war. Eight months later the position had changed to 4.64 which is more favorable to war than was the original attitude. Probably other influences had played upon the children during these eight months. In all other cases residual traces of the exposure were in evidence at the end of periods of two and one-half, four, six, or eight months.

The principle of permanence is indicated by these investigations. One cannot say that the effects of pictures disappear rapidly. And this position is supported in numerous cases reported by Blumer from the movie autobiographies of his subjects, where hundreds of memories of the influence of specific pictures are related in later years by adults. In other cases Blumer's autobiographers, however, attest to the short-lived influence of movies upon conduct. This trio of conclusions has great significance for education. We can conclude on the basis of fact that single pictures may produce a change in attitude, that the influence of pictures is cumulative, and that their effects are substantially permanent. This is the second link in the chain of evidence.

How to interpret the social significance of these changes is an interesting consideration. One clue is given in the scores upon the scales. For instance, to select one of the more powerful films, before the picture "Son of the Gods" was shown there were individuals in the group at one extreme position of unfavorableness marked 9.5 upon the scale—meaning roughly: "There are no refined or cultured Chinese," "I don't see how any one could ever like the Chinese," or "There is nothing about the Chinese that I like or admire." Six steps to the other extreme in this group were those who held: "I like the Chinese" and "I'd like to know more Chinese people." The mode of the group and the average were slightly unfavorable at 6.72, which is slightly beyond the neutral point of 6 and toward the unfavorable end. The mode (the most common position taken by the individuals in the group) was: "I have no particular love nor hate for the Chinese." After the picture was shown the same spread of six units was in evidence, from 3.5 to 9.5, but there were fewer children at 9.5 and more at 3.5. The change was 1.22 indicating a shift of about 20 per cent of the distance between the positions of the most extreme and the least extreme individuals in the group. The mode had shifted from neutrality to a point between "The Chinese are pretty decent" and "Chinese parents are unusually devoted to their children."

STIMULATING EMOTIONS

LABORATORY techniques and autobiographical case studies were utilized in studying the effect of motion pictures upon the emotions of children. Dysinger and Ruckmick worked with a galvanometer to measure galvanic responses and with the pneumo-cardiograph to measure changes in the circulatory system. They [7] worked with 89 subjects in their laboratory and with 61 subjects in the theaters. In age the subjects ranged from six years to fifty and were divided between those under 11 years; 11 to 12 years; 13 to 15 years; 16 to 18 years; 19 to 25 years; and over 25 years. In the theater under theater conditions they used 61 subjects in three age groups: around 9 years, 16 years, and 22 years. Children of average intelligence were chosen with intelligence quotients between 90 and 110 when available, or with normal age-grade placement in other cases. The subjects were about equally divided between the sexes.

The apparatus was attached to the 150 individual children in the laboratory and in the balcony or the rear seats of theaters. The customary patience of the psychological laboratory technician was amply exercised in this investigation. The records of the reactions of the subjects were taken on films. In numerous cases verbal reports were given by the subject about the points of greatest interest to serve as explanations of the records.

Two types of scene were used: those that depicted dangerous situations and those that contained sex content. In the laboratory the pictures "Hop to it Bell Hop," a slap-

---

[7] *The Emotional Responses of Children to the Motion-Picture Situation*, by W. S. Dysinger and Christian A. Ruckmick.

stick, "The Iron Mule," a comedy, and "The Feast of Ishtar," an erotic play, were used. In the theaters the subjects viewed "Charlie Chan's Chance," "The Yellow Ticket," "The Road to Singapore," and "His Woman." The reactions of subjects at 187 points for scenes of danger, conflict, or tragedy and at 35 points for suggestive or love scenes were recorded.

The specific contribution to this type of study lies in the fact that the apparatus records very fine reactions when the subject is sitting quietly—looking like a well-mannered, quiet, and well-controlled young boy or girl. It reinforces the impression that one cannot estimate from gross movement of the body or absence of such movement what is happening to an individual. Specifically, it cannot be inferred by a parent sitting beside his quiet child that internal excitement is not occurring as incidents in the screen drama unfold before him.

Among the findings the most significant are three in number. The records show first that scenes of danger, conflict, or tragedy produce the greatest effect as measured by the galvanometer upon the 9 year old group (from 6 to 12 years old); the curve falls rapidly among the 16 year olds (from 13 to 18 years) and is weakest with the adult group (over 19 years). There is a real difference in the reactions from one age level to the next. The reaction of adults is small compared with that of the 9 year olds because of their consciousness of the unreality of the scenes, the quality of the acting, or their ability to forecast what is going to happen.

The records show a second trend in connection with the romantic and erotic scenes. In this case the 9 year olds (6 to 12 years old) are on the average least affected. To be sure, their deflections on the graph are similar in average to those of the adults in one series of experiments and greater than adults in the other; but the investigators point out the likelihood that the danger elements, which in some cases could not be completely eliminated from erotic scenes, account for part of the deflections and this is the more likely because children of this age, according to Holaday and Stoddard, remember only one half to two thirds of what they see and may, therefore, misunderstand some of the scenes. This element of misunderstanding was frequently discovered by Dysinger and Ruckmick among the younger children in their interviews.

The greatest deflections from normal patterns in viewing erotic scenes was located among the 16 year olds (ages 12 to 18). The average is the largest of the three age levels. They are most often extreme, and verbal reports in the interviews seldom mention the factors which influence adults called "adult discount"—the factor of realizing the unreality of the drama, observing the quality of the acting, and the like. Compared with the other groups the 16 year old group gives the most extreme responses.

More specifically the authors report: "Most children of 9 gave very little response [to love scenes]. At 10 some were found to respond. At 11 and 12 others responded. Above 13 there was usually a definite response. The peak in intensity of reaction does not seem to be reached until the age of 16 years."

A third result reported frequently by the investigator is the presence of striking individual differences in children. In "The Feast of Ishtar," for instance, twelve erotic "reading points" were studied. In the 6 to 10 year group two subjects gave only one reading, each above zero. (Zero indicates a merely normal reaction.) However, one boy of 9 years and 2 months gave only one zero reading. He was affected by all the scenes but one. Between these two extremes were others who gave significant responses. Similarly in the 11 to 12 year group one subject gave only zero readings, while another provided only two zero readings. Again in the 13 to 15 year group one subject gave zero readings at all points except where the index was zero-plus, in contrast to another subject only five months older, who gave wide deflections at all the points. In the 16 to 18 year group at 125 reading points there were only 16 zero readings. Here again, however, the subject least affected reacted with seven zero readings in contrast with another who showed violent reactions in all. In the adult group there were many more zero readings than in the 16 year group but a considerable number of large deflections were also found. Similar individual differences were found in the reaction of individuals at all ages to scenes of danger. While in general the reactions to these scenes decreased with age, marked differences were found even among the adults.

It thus appears that while children of ages 6 to 12 are on the average not likely to react to love scenes, individual children in the group will show significant reactions and similarly the 13 to 15 year group will contain individuals who show important reactions. In the 16 to 18 year group it appears that none is free from the influence of love scenes.

A fourth indication of interest is the conclusion of the investigators that there are in this study no clear sex differences in reaction to love scenes. Males and females are equally influenced. Differences within each sex are greater than differences between the sexes.

The Dysinger-Ruckmick study in general establishes the fact that measurable reactions of children to two types of scene—danger and love—can be secured and indicates the significant social conclusion that a few children at the age of nine years react to erotic scenes in motion pictures, and that this reaction occurs in increasing numbers of children until it reaches its climax among the 16 to 18 year olds and thereafter falls away probably through the influence of "adult discount."

By a quite different technique Blumer studied the effects of motion pictures upon the emotional life of children. In seeking to throw light upon this problem Blumer used motion-picture autobiographies supplemented by interviews. The autobiographies were secured from about 1,800 college and high-school students, office workers, and factory workers. Four types of experience were studied: fright, sorrow, love, and excitement. Stating his conclusions in relation to the emotion of fright as typical of the influence of motion pictures upon the four areas, Blumer says that the experience "of fright, horror, or agony as a result of witnessing certain kinds of motion pictures seems common from the accounts of children and of high-school and college students. The experience is most conspicuous in the case of children although it is not infrequently showed by those of greater age. Its manifestations vary from shielding the eyes at crucial scenes during the showing of the pictures to nightmares and terrifying dreams, including sometimes experiences of distinct shock, almost of neurotic proportions."

The extent of the fright among children is "quite large." Of 237 children in the fourth to seventh grades in one school who were asked if they had ever been frightened or horrified by any motion picture 93 per cent answered in the affirmative. Of 458 high-school students who wrote autobiographies 61 per cent mentioned such experiences and 17 per cent said they never had been frightened by pictures.

Among the movie objects which produce fear in the young

are: "spooks, ghosts, phantoms, devils, gorillas, bears, tigers, bandits, 'bad men,' grabbing hands and claws, fighting, shooting, falling or hanging from high places, drownings, wrecks, collisions, fire, and flood." Expressions of emotions during the witnessing of fearful pictures are such as: biting finger nails, crunching teeth, twisting caps, grabbing one's neighbor, feeling shivery, hiding the eyes until the scene changes, looking away, screaming, jumping out of the seat, and getting under the seat. On the way home fear so induced leads to such actions as: running home, being frightened at shadows, avoiding dark streets, and holding on to others. At home the effects appear as: staying close to mother, looking back of one's chair, fear of going to bed, looking under the bed, closing the window, begging for a light to be left burning, hiding the head under covers, seeing devils dancing in the dark, wanting to sleep with some one, bad dreams, calling out in sleep, sleepwalking, and the like.

Such expressions of fright are ordinarily short-lived. The child regains control of his thoughts and feelings with the passage of time, sometimes by the next day, sometimes in the course of the next few days. But in the case of some individuals fear or fright becomes fixed and lasts for a long time. Blumer does not assess the value or harm of showing such pictures to children and points to the interesting fact that many children like to be frightened by pictures.

Blumer concludes that the sampling of instances of fright, sorrow, love, and excitement provided in his report "suffice to establish the point that motion pictures may play very vividly upon a given emotion of the individual; his impulses may be so aroused and his imagery so fixed that for a period of time he is transported out of his normal conduct and is completely subjugated by his impulses."

These studies establish the third link in the chain of evidence. Holaday and Stoddard show that much information is secured from motion pictures, Peterson and Thurstone establish the forceful influence of a single picture upon attitudes, and Dysinger and Ruckmick and Blumer indicate the considerable influence of the movies upon the emotions of children.

AFFECTING SLEEP

THE investigators had two alternatives to consider in studying the possible effects of motion-picture attendance upon health. One was to investigate the direct relationship between movie attendance and health by correlating it with the various physiological indices of health. The other was to study the correlation of theater attendance with motility in sleep and assume an established relationship between the disturbance of sleep patterns and the indices of health. The latter alternative was chosen.

Renshaw, Miller, and Marquis [8] undertook this investigation. Specifically they selected children, ascertained their normal sleep patterns in terms of motility, exposed the children to the movies, and observed the changes in sleep patterns which followed movie attendance. To secure comparative data they measured changes occurring after sleep deprivation in the evening and in the morning, and after drinking coffee or Kaffee Hag in the evening.

To locate children with regular régimes of living in such numbers as to permit of economical study, whose actions could be controlled, and who were near a theater was a difficult task which was fortunately solved by the coöperation of the officials of the Bureau of Juvenile Research in Columbus, Ohio. Briefly the children were of all types,

[8] *Children's Sleep,* by Samuel Renshaw, Vernon L. Miller, and Dorothy P. Marquis.

"good" and "bad," "bright" and "dull," varying in age
from 6 to 19 years, and living under conditions which produce normal happiness.

In the nine experiments conducted by the investigators,
92 boys and 71 girls were used varying in age from 6 to
19. Seventy-five per cent were between the ages of
9.5 and 16.5. The investigators state that because of the
care in selection of the subjects they "feel justified in in-
ferring that the experimental children represent a fair sampling of an average child population and that the regularity
of the conditions of living at the Bureau favors rather than
calls into question the general applicability of the conclusions" based upon their experimental results.

The apparatus was interesting. Children were studied
in groups of ten boys and of ten girls. Beneath the single
bed of each child was attached a hypnograph unit which
caused an electrical contact to break whenever the occu-
pant of the bed moved slightly. The hypnograph was con-
nected by wire with a polygraph unit which on rolls of
paper provided records of the periods of quiescence and
motility of each child.

In all 163 children were used. Records were kept for 347
nights in nine experiments. This produced a total of 6,650
child nights of sleep—equivalent in mere amount to 18
years of study of one child.

The first step in each experiment was to establish a
stable sleep pattern for each hour of the night for each
child. The investigators found that the hourly motility
distribution is a characteristic that is stable to a high degree
under normal routine living undisturbed by illness, emotional upsets, etc. Incidentally the average child aged 6 to
18 stirs or rearranges his position once each 8.7 minutes.

The normal sleep pattern having been established for

each subject at the beginning of each experiment, the children left the Bureau at 6:20 P.M.; were taken on foot in orderly fashion to a neighborhood theater; returned by 8:45; and were in bed promptly at 9:00. In all they saw 58 pictures which happened to be showing on the nights they attended.

The experiments exhibited a variety of forms. For instance one series consisted of ten normal nights, ten movie nights, and five normal nights. Another distribution was: fourteen normal nights, six movies in two weeks to approximate the distribution and frequency of attendance of many average children, and eight normal nights.

Children were also taken on interesting trips, as a substitute for movie going, to check against the hypothesis that measurable results of movie attendance may be due to a "holiday effect." The influence of humidity and temperature on sleep patterns was investigated. And as has been indicated the children were on certain controlled occasions provided with coffee and Kaffee Hag at the evening meal and at 8:30 P.M. They were on occasion kept up until 12:00 at night and again asked to rise three hours earlier in the morning than usual to compare the resulting sleep patterns with those that followed movie attendance. (The children considered all these experiments as thrilling adventures for which they felt they were fortunate to be selected.)

For our purposes three significant findings stand out in these studies.

First, increase in motility following the movies ranged from 0 to 90 per cent. On the average boys showed 26 per cent and girls 14 per cent greater hourly motility after movies than in normal sleep. Twenty-five per cent increase is equivalent approximately to pushing an 8 year old boy until he is as restless in sleep as a 12 year old normally is. The boys and girls are more restless than they normally should be. To these increases are to be added cases of children who show symptoms of fatigue in the form of decreased motility which according to the scientific literature is equally important as a measure of fatigue. The effect of movie attendance is measured by deviations from normal sleep in both directions—increased and decreased motility.

Second, 50 per cent of the boys show half as much or more change from the normal after seeing all types of movies as they show following enforced sitting up for three additional hours from 9:00 to midnight. On the average, a boy who went to the movies and was in bed by nine in the evening was as restless in sleep as if he had sat up until midnight before going to bed. Many individuals showed even greater change after certain impressive pictures. Movie influence was persistent beyond the movie night and was dependent upon the age, sex, and mental "set" of the child. Continued sleep deprivation in the mornings or evenings produced disciplinary conditions so serious that the matrons asked that the sleep deprivation experiments be discontinued. Matinee attendance would probably show as great an effect as night attendance or even greater.

These facts indicate the conclusion that parents who allow their children to go to a movie should do so with the knowledge that the experience is about as disturbing to sleep patterns as sitting up till midnight or that the influence of some pictures on motility is as great on some children as the drinking of two cups of coffee in the evening.

Third, numerous variations in the effects of the movies to modify the averages were observed by the investigators. Notably some pictures are much more disturbing to sleep patterns than others. Equally significant, some children are much more affected by some pictures than are other children. In general the sleep motility of children below ten is affected less by attendance from 6:30 to 8:30 in the evening than is that of older children. But again there are exceptions and variations.

The investigators summarize: "We can conclude, however, from our results that seeing *some* films does induce a disturbance of relaxed, recuperative sleep in children to a degree which, if indulged in with sufficient frequency, can be regarded as detrimental to normal health and growth. We do not believe that any sweeping generalizations can be made about the 'type' of film or 'type' of child most likely to be influenced. There is a distinct need for careful intensive study on individual children's reactions to movies."

Thus it appears that movies selected unwisely and indulged in intemperately will have a detrimental effect upon the health of children. This is the fourth link in the chain of evidence.

INFLUENCING CONDUCT

CONDUCT is a product of many factors. Of these factors the preceding investigations have explored four. We may assume the obvious position that information is a factor in behavior: what one knows determines in part what one does. We may also assume that attitudes toward social objects affect conduct: if one is friendly toward an objective of action in a situation he will be influenced to build one behavior pattern; if unfriendly, to build another. It may also be fairly assumed that experiences which are accompanied by excitement and emotion have a more powerful effect upon conduct than do those which are placid and uninteresting. Likewise, we may assume that fatigue expressed either by increased or decreased sleep motility results in producing a tone of behavior by which conduct patterns are affected. We have seen that motion pictures have an influence upon all of these factors.

We were able to check the validity of these assumptions, which square with common sense, by a mass of evidence from the studies of Blumer and his associates. Here it was possible to secure hundreds of cases in which the information and attitudes acquired in the movies were directly operative in the conduct of children.

Blumer, Thrasher, and their associates [9] supplemented the foregoing indirect studies of conduct by investigating the direct relationships existing between movies and conduct. Blumer used an autobiography technique, supplemented by interviews, accounts of conversations, and questionnaires. His major study was based upon the case reports of 634 students in two universities, 481 college and junior-college students in four colleges, 583 high-school students, 67 office workers, and 58 factory workers. After studying many biographies written without specific directions and discovering the patterns into which they unconsciously fell, he formulated a few questions to guide the writers as follows: trace the history of your interest in the movies; describe how motion pictures have affected your emotions and your moods; write fully about what you have imitated from the movies; describe your experience with pictures of love and romance; write fully about any ambitions and temptations you have gotten from the movies. Unusual care was taken to preserve the anonymity of the writers. Interviews were held with 81 university students who had previously written autobiographies and 54 high-school students who had not. Careful accounts of con-

---

[9] *Movies and Conduct*, by Herbert Blumer; *Movies, Delinquency, and Crime*, by Herbert Blumer and Philip M. Hauser; *Boys, Movies, and City Streets*, by Paul G. Cressey and Frederick M. Thrasher.

versations were secured from several fraternities, several sororities, and girls' groups and from several cliques of high-school boys and girls, from conversations of high-school boys and girls at parties, and from boys' gangs, play groups, office girls, and factory workers. Direct questionnaires were administered to 1,200 children in the fifth and sixth grades of 12 public schools in Chicago distributed between schools in high, medium, and low delinquency areas. One set of questionnaires was filled out by a special school for truants and boys with behavior problems. Direct observations were made of children while in attendance at small neighborhood theaters.

From these sources a huge mass of materials was collected. The materials were analyzed to discover trends and significant facts. The main use of the material "has been to show and illuminate the different kinds of ways in which motion pictures touch the lives of young people." Experiences which recurred with a high rate of frequency in the separate documents were selected and samples of each type were presented in the report.

Obviously the validity of personal reports is an issue that has a bearing upon the conclusions of the investigators. Upon this question Blumer took all known precautions against error and presents the following facts about the safeguards which they threw around the investigations: (1) Machinery was set up to demonstrate in an obvious manner the anonymity of the written accounts. (2) The utmost care and attention were devoted to gaining full coöperation from the students in securing their frank, honest, and unexaggerated statements. (3) The interviews held six months after the autobiographies were written were used in the cases of some 60 students with their consent but without this previous knowledge as a check against agreement between the content of the written report and the substance of the interview; no discrepancy of importance was discovered. (4) The accounts were checked for internal consistency and some twenty which showed contradiction were discarded. (5) Conversations were checked against the written reports. (6) Individuals were asked to write only about those experiences which they recalled vividly.

The chief means of checking the character of the experiences given in the written documents was "in the comparison of document with document. The accounts were written independently by students in different schools and localities. . . . The comparison of large numbers of documents coming from different groups of people with no knowledge of each other made it possible to ascertain the general run of experiences. The contents of documents coming from different sources yielded substantially the same general kind of experiences."

In short the validity of the report is determined by the care taken to secure valid materials and by the mass and consistency of testimony bearing upon significant issues. This mass and consistency protects the validity of the conclusions.

Foremost among the contributions of these reports is the elaboration of the phenomenon of "emotional possession" which is characteristic of the experience of children before the motion-picture screen. Watching in the dark of the theater, the young child sits in the presence of reality when he observes the actors perform and the plot of the drama unfold. He sees the actions of people living in a real world— not of actors playing a make-believe rôle. His emotions are aroused in ways that have been described. He forgets his surroundings. He loses ordinary control of his feelings, his actions, and his thoughts. He identifies himself with the plot and loses himself in the picture. His "emotional condition may get such a strong grip on him that even his efforts to rid himself of it by reasoning with himself may prove of little avail." He is possessed by the drama.

The intensity of child experience in viewing pictures cannot be fully appreciated by adults. To adults the picture is good or bad, the acting satisfactory or unsatisfactory, the singing up to or not up to standard. To them a picture is just a picture. They may recall memories of thrills they used to have but the memories are pale in comparison to the actual experience. They get a more vivid impression of this excitement by watching a theater full of children as a thrilling drama unreels. They see the symptoms of keen emotion. But even in the presence of these manifestations they miss the depth and intensity of the child's experience.

Several factors contribute to emotional possession. The actions and the setting are concrete. When in the fairy story the child is told that the prince led his troops into battle he has to provide his own imagery; but in the picture he sees the charming prince at the head of a band of "real" men. Every significant visual image is provided before his eyes in the motion picture. He does not have to translate the words in which the story is conveyed. He sees machines; he does not hear about them. He visits the islands of the southern seas in a real ship; he does not have to listen to a narrator describe the scenes in words alone. The motion picture tells a very concrete and simple tale in a fashion which makes the story easy to grasp.

Emotional possession is also caused by the dramatic forms of the picture. One of the objectives of drama is to arouse the emotions. Indeed, the weakness of many "teaching films" is the absence of dramatic elements—often necessarily omitted because of the nature of the content to be taught. But in the commercial movies and in teaching films of action, the dramatic flow of the story stirs the emotions and produces that intensity of experience which Blumer calls "emotional possession."

A third factor which contributes its influence to this condition is the attractiveness of the pictures—beautiful and thrilling scenes, interesting people, attractive persons moving on the stage, stimulating colors, expert lighting, and the like. The child wants to be a part of such a bit of life. He does not pull back from the experience; he hurls himself into it.

All of these factors and probably others produce a condition that is favorable to certain types of learning. This is the quality of authority. Children accept as true, correct, proper, right what they see on the screen. They have little knowledge. The people on the screen are confidence-producing. Everything works to build up a magnificent and impressive world. Holaday and Stoddard found the children accepting both fact and error as fact. Blumer indicates the power of movie patterns upon conduct. The authority of the screen may account for some of the striking change of attitude of children found by Peterson and Thurstone.

All of these considerations lead inevitably to the increasing strength of the conclusion that the motion picture is an extremely powerful medium of education.

A second conclusion drawn from the report is that the range of influence of movies is very wide. Blumer found in studying two thousand children what every parent knows about his own child—that the movies dominate the patterns of play of children in a wide variety of forms. He presents scores of cases to show that the world of phantasy of young children and adolescents and of both sexes is ruled by movie subjects. Dozens of cases are presented to show the effects of the movies in stimulating emotions of fright, sorrow, love, and "excitement." Cases are presented to illustrate how the movies give children techniques of action in situations which are of interest to them ranging from the trivial techniques of the playground to disturbing cues for the delinquent. And most far-reaching of all he indicates how they stir powerful ambitions, good and bad; develop permanent ideals, high and low; and crystallize the framework of life careers. In most unexpected quarters the influence of the movies is discovered in the reports of Blumer and Thrasher and their associates.

A third concept which supplements emotional possession and range of influence is the guidance concept which grows out of the preceding paragraph. Children are born into a world of which they know nothing. They are little individualists who have laboriously to learn how to fit into social groups. They possess impulses, instincts, wishes, desires, which drive them on to seek experience, adventure, and satisfaction. They are avidly interested in everything that seems to them to be able to provide what they want.

Yet they know so little and are so anxious to learn. They seek information, stimulation, and guidance in every direction. They are often confused, frequently maladjusted, and sometimes without confidence. In this situation the motion picture seems to be a godsend to them. While they are being entertained they are being shown in attractive and authoritative fashion what to do. They are guided in one direction or another as they absorb rightly or wrongly this idea or that one. Sometimes the guidance is good, at other times it is bad. Sometimes it lies in a direction opposed to the teachings of the home or the school; at other times it reinforces them. But always the motion picture is potentially a powerfully influential director. Not the only guide which leads them, to be sure: the community, chums and playmates, the home, the school, the church, the newspapers, all are used by these omnivorous seekers after the kinds of experience they want. But among them the motion picture possesses potency so substantial that society must not fail to understand and see that it is used beneficently in the guidance of children.

One means of helping the child to dominate his movie experiences rather than be possessed emotionally by them is a fourth product of these investigations. It is possible to increase control of movie experiences by developing what Ruckmick calls adult discount and Blumer describes as emotional detachment. Blumer describes one interesting series of cases to show the stages of growth of this maturer attitude. Certain fourth graders showed in the most undisguised fashion a great interest in serial thrillers and particularly in one. They talked freely and spoke with frank enthusiasm. The sixth graders were reluctant to talk. They admitted interest yet felt some shame at their interest in a "childish" picture. Their attitude was one of affected sophistication. The attitude of the eighth graders was, however, one of spontaneous and frank disapproval, dislike, and disgust at serials. The steps were three in number, frank approval, affected sophistication, and mature disapproval.

Three methods of developing adult discount or emotional detachment are mentioned by Blumer. The one most commonly present in the evolution of children's attitudes is the response to the attitude of slightly older groups or the "sophisticated" members of one's own group—as just indicated. The child is quick to put away childish things when his group frowns upon them as childish and he enjoys exhibiting superiority and sophistication. In later years and with wider experience adult discount may be produced by a second factor: the conviction that the pictures are not true to life. "In real life things aren't that way." This is a normal method of developing sophistication. The third method is to give children instruction about the movies. Sometimes Blumer found that talks with parents, or suggestions that "this is only make believe" from older people, helped the children to develop emotional detachment. Particularly, however, detachment comes with learning how pictures are made, how effects are secured, what to look for in pictures, what makes pictures artistically good or bad. Dale's appreciation study contributes to this end.

In summary of the direct influences of motion pictures on conduct: they owe their power over children chiefly to the factor of emotional possession; the range of influence of commercial movies is very wide; the motion picture because of its potency in many directions plays a substantial and significant rôle in the informal guidance of children; and the influence of pictures can be controlled in considerable measure by the development of emotional detachment and the application of an adult discount. In producing this intelligent attitude toward the movies, instruction in motion-picture criticism and appreciation provides a promising lead.

With this section, we have concluded a description of the studies which essayed to measure the influence of the motion picture as such. We see that as an instrument of education it has unusual power to impart information, to influence specific attitudes toward objects of social value, to affect emotions either in gross or in microscopic proportions, to affect health in a minor degree through sleep disturbance, and to affect profoundly the patterns of conduct of children.

It is now appropriate to examine the content of current

movies and discover the directions in which they are probably
leading attitudes and conduct.

ATTENDING THE MOVIES

IN calculating the effect of commercial movies upon
children it is necessary to know the extent to which children
are exposed to them. This information was collected by
Dale [10] in two forms: the attendance of children per week
and the percentage of children found in audiences.

The attendance per week was estimated by studying
the reports of 55,000 children from the kindergarten through
the twelfth grade in 44 representative communities in Ohio
and three communities outside the state. His study was
checked against 18 other studies previously made (but none
so large nor so carefully conducted) and all were found to
give slightly larger numbers than his.

The attendance data were gathered directly from school
children above the third grade on printed blanks and from
younger children by interviews. The validity of the information so obtained was checked by three techniques
and found to be satisfactory.

The children were asked to state how often they attended
the movies during the preceding seven days and the weeks
were scattered throughout the school year. Dale found
that among children from 5 to 8 the average attendance
per week was .42 times and that 22 per cent never attend.
The average boy of age 5 to 8 attends 24 picture programs
a year and the average girl 19. In the age range 8 to 19 the
average attendance was .99 or approximately once a week
and only 5 per cent never attend. The average boy in this
range attends 57 picture programs a year and the average
girl 46 in the same period.

[10] *Children's Attendance at Motion Pictures*, by Edgar Dale.

Children above 7 years of age on the average attend the movies once a week. In the age range 8 to 19, 27 per cent of the boys and 21 per cent of the girls attend twice or more. Children in rural areas attend less frequently than urban children.

It was found that fathers take their boys of ages 8 to 19 very infrequently—2.63 per cent of all cases. Mothers accompany their sons about 3.65 per cent of the times and this percentage drops almost consistently from attendance with 8 year olds to 19 year olds. Boys of 8 are accompanied by both parents 23 per cent of the times they attend. Brothers or sisters accompany each other·to the movies in 14.81 per cent of the cases. The percentage of brother-sister attendance remains stationary from 8 to 11 years at about 22 per cent and drops steadily to 4.43 per cent at 18. Going with some one else averages 11.45 per cent. It steadily rises from 8 to 17 years of age with a plateau thereafter. Going by one's self remains fairly constant around an average of 25 per cent, except for the 8 and 9 year olds, who go alone less often.

Fathers go with girls on exactly the same percentage of occasions as they go with boys. Mothers attend nearly three times as often with daughters as with sons and with 8 year old daughters one third of the times they go. The percentage falls for mothers consistently thereafter. In girls' attendance with own friends the curves closely resemble the boys'. With "some one else" they go more frequently and by themselves only one third as often as the boys. The order of frequency for boys from frequent to infrequent is: own friends, alone, brother or sister, some one else, both parents, mother, and father. For girls it runs: own friends, brother or sister, some one else, mother, alone, and father.

About 80 per cent of the boys and girls stay in the theater for only one showing. About 18 per cent of boys and girls see the feature through twice. About 20 per cent of the boys see the news reel through twice and 26 per cent the comedy twice. The girls stay somewhat less often for these. One per cent of boys and girls stay three times for feature, news reel, and comedy. Only 2 per cent of the girls reporting attend the theaters in the mornings. In the afternoons 33 per cent are found in attendance. From the age of 13 to 19 the percentages drop from 38 to 14. In the evenings the average attendance for girls is 64 per cent. To the age of 13 the percentages of evening attendance cluster around 55. Thereafter they rise slowly to 84 for the 19 year olds. The boys' figures are approximately the same.

In general for children of both sexes the attendance in the morning is negligible, in the afternoon about one third; in the evenings two thirds of the children's attendance is found. The most popular days of the week are Saturday, 34 per cent, Sunday, 27 per cent, and Friday, 12 per cent. The average of the other days of the week is approximately 7 per cent.

The proportion of children in the theater audience was based upon the Columbus study. Attendance was clocked at 15 representative theaters out of a total of 43 theaters in the city. The audience entering was classified by trained observers into four age groups: under 7, 8 to 13, 14 to 20, and 21 and over. The study was scattered over approximately three months with about 240,000 persons in attendance per week.

It was found that 3.1 per cent of those entering the theaters were under seven years of age; 7 to 13 years of age, 13.7 per cent; 14 to 20 years, 20.8 per cent; and 21 or over, 62.4 per cent. Thus approximately 17 per cent of the audiences were grade-school children and 37 per cent were minors. The percentage of children under 14 years found in audiences in different types of theater ran as follows: good neighborhood, 27.9; poor neighborhood, 23.3; good all-Negro, 14.7; poor downtown, 8.0; and good downtown, 5.5. It is of interest to note that at all ages there were more males than females in the audiences. At ages 7 to 13 the proportion of boys to girls was 64 to 36; at ages 14 to 20, 57 to 43; and above 20, 59 to 41.

Calculations based upon these studies and other data led Dale to the conclusion that there were in weekly attendance at theaters throughout the nation 11,000,000 children under 14 years of age and 28,000,000 minors.

From this study of attendance it can be conservatively concluded that 11,000,000 children attend motion pictures once a week, that 17 per cent of the audiences are made up of children under 14 years of age, and that 37 per cent are minors. Obviously, whether or not these figures are exact within a million or so, it may be concluded if one notes the age spread of attendance that children are exposed to all the films that are shown in commercial theaters.

The content of the pictures thus becomes a matter of deep concern to parents. If the commercial movies reinforce the training of the home, the school, and the church, parents have cause for deep satisfaction. If they conflict with the teachings of these agencies parents who believe in the teachings of the home, the school, and the church will be seriously disturbed. Light is thrown upon this critical question by the studies of Dale, Peters, Blumer, Thrasher, and their associates.

THE CONTENT OF CURRENT MOVIES

THE influences of commercial movies are felt in many directions. They provide entertainment in agreeable theater surroundings for millions of people. They display beautiful scenes from all parts of the world. The action of the drama is rapid and often thrilling. Movies have a marked effect upon wearing apparel and social manners. They provide romance for millions who feel little of romance in their daily lives.

These contributions of the commercial movies are fully recognized by thoughtful people. Our investigations, however, concerned themselves only incidentally with phases of the motion picture that did not directly influence the attitudes and conduct of children. No attention in a major degree was paid to their effects upon adults, which is quite another problem to be solved in the light of many considerations which are not germane to the problem of influence upon children. Theoretically the commercial movies might be quite unobjectionable for seasoned adults and still be quite unsuitable for children. Adults are mature and accepted judges of what they choose to see. But toward children American society has taken a protective attitude. Knowing that children are immature, society is convinced that the experiences to which they are exposed should be selected to produce beneficial results upon character and conduct. American society is deeply concerned about the moral influences which surround its young.

Turning to the content of commercial pictures and viewing it against this background, we find that Dale [11] analyzed the themes of 500 feature pictures shown in each of the years 1920, 1925, and 1930 with the aid of the Harrison Reports. In conducting his analysis he discovered 10 classes of theme: crime, sex, love, comedy, mystery, war, children (about children or for children), history, travel, and social propaganda. The pictures were classified by individual readers. The judgment of each reader

[11] *The Content of Motion Pictures*, by Edgar Dale.

was checked in samplings of 100 pictures shown in each of the three years by having three readers classify each of the 300 pictures. The three readers agreed in nine out of ten cases, which was sufficiently close agreement to establish approximate reliability of the judgment of each reader. When there was more than one theme in a picture it was allocated to the class to which the major theme belonged.

The Big Three among the themes in 1930 were: love 29.6 per cent, crime 27.4 per cent, and sex 15.0 per cent, making a total of 72 per cent of all themes. That is, in 1930 approximately 7 out of 10 pictures exhibited one of the Big Three as their major themes. The percentages of themes in 1920, 1925, and 1930 were substantially the same except for the theme of love. The love percentages in 1920, 1925, and 1930 were respectively the following: 44.6, 32.8, and 29.6. For crime pictures the following percentages occurred in the same years: 24.0, 29.6, and 27.4; and for sex: 13.0, 16.8, and 15.0. Comedy aggregating 16 per cent in 1930 and mystery and war, together totaling 8.6 per cent, followed the Big Three. The other four classes divided the remaining pictures, 3.4 per cent, among them: out of 500 pictures in 1930 one was a children's picture, seven were historical films, nine were travel pictures, and no social-propaganda picture was included.

An analysis of the Big Three was conducted by the investigator. Under the 27.4 per cent of crime pictures was included those dealing in a major way with: blackmailing; extortion; injury, hate, and revenge—the idea of vengeance—feuds; corruption in politics or business, bribery, swindling, crook plays, criminal activity predominant; racketeers, bootleggers, gamblers, gangsters, smugglers, thieves; outlaws, bandits, rustlers—"western" type—holdups, gun fighting, etc., being the main interest; and criminal types and activities—prison stories. When one goes to the movies once a week he sees on the average one such picture a little oftener than once a month.

The criminals are not frequently starred as attractive characters. In almost two thirds of the cases adults classify them as unattractive; how children classify them was not discovered. Dale says, "It is evident, however, that movie criminals are not always shown as low, cowardly, weak-minded, and physically repulsive. The evidence strongly suggests that no small proportion of the criminals are accomplished in some of the social graces and many are well-dressed. Not infrequently we see on the screen criminals who are courageous and meet danger fearlessly."

When the pictures present the solution for the crime problem presented in a picture the investigator says, "The fundamental philosophy of movie criminology is that the crimes are committed by bad people. Therefore, jail or deport the criminals and the crime problem is solved."

In 115 pictures selected at random in 1932 as they appeared in the theaters of Columbus, Ohio, some interesting details were analyzed. Fifty-nine of the 115 pictures showed killing techniques of a wide variety. This is at the rate of approximately one in every other picture. In 45, killings occurred, and in 21, killings were attempted. The revolver was used in 22 pictures, knifing in 9, general shooting in 5. In less than 5 pictures each were shown: hanging, stabbing, beating to death, drowning, lynching, machine-gunning, strangling, and eight other methods, making a total of 18 varieties of exits from the movie scenes of action.

Out of 115 pictures analyzed and the 59 pictures of these in which killings occurred or were attempted, the heroine slipped three times in attempts to kill and got her man only once. Heroines in movie tradition, like kings in chess, are to be protected. The heroes, however, were in 14 tight places where lethal weapons were needed, and they did much better jobs than the heroines. They were successful in 13 out of 14 tries. The villains came oftener to bat than the heroes, but with a lower batting average. They made only 22 hits out of 42 times at bat, with a percentage of .524—the heroes' percentage was .929. The lady villains were responsible for 8 murders. The rest of the carnage was contributed by other men and women in the casts.

This is a rather sorry layout for the children to see when they go to the movies. One out of four of 'all the films are crime pictures and crimes are committed in many more than those in which they are the central theme.

Pictures of sex constitute 15 per cent of the 500 pictures studied for 1930. In this class are listed pictures whose major themes are: living together without marriage being apparent; loose living, impropriety known or implied; plot revolving around seduction, adultery, kept women, illegitimate children the central characters, sex situations; "women for sale" stuff; bedroom farce with incidents on the fringes of sexual impropriety. Among the 115 pictures analyzed in detail, 22 (or one out of five) presented illicit love as a goal of 35 leading characters: the heroes (4); the heroines (3); the villains (11) the villainesses (7); and other men and women (10).

Romantic love pictures (29.6 per cent in 1930) include in the class: love against a background of thrills, suspense, or melodrama; courtship, love, flirtations, marital difficulties; historical romance; operetta type, colorful scenes and songs. Some of these are beautiful and in good taste, others are sensual and in conflict with the mores of every group studied by Peters. Blumer has shown how techniques of love-making are learned by the adolescents. He and Ruckmick have shown the intense emotional possession experienced by the 16 year olds. They eat them up, and 3 out of 10 pictures present the major theme of love. The 72 per cent devoted to the Big Three produce an unbalanced diet for the children to digest. Occasional pictures of these sorts can be vigorously defended. But 7 out of 10 provide a diet too narrow for the welfare of children.

The goals attempted by the characters throw further light on the content of the pictures. Here the investigator sought in 115 pictures to classify the goals of the leading characters. In all 883 goals were detected. Winning another's love constituted 18 per cent; and marriage for love, 8 per cent; illicit love, 4 per cent; conquering a rival, 2 per cent; protection of loved one, 2 per cent—a total of 34 per cent goals of love. The range extended to other goals— professional success, revenge, crime for gain, performance of duty, financial success, and a very large class of goals not easy to classify constituting 29 per cent of the total.

A number of analyses of specific details are relevant to the question. Of these one is selected. Dale found that in the 115 pictures analyzed, 90, or 78 per cent, or four out of five, contained liquor situations. In 49 of the 115, or in 43 per cent, intoxication was shown. In 43 per cent of the cases the hero drank and in 23 per cent the heroine imbibed. The villains and the "lady" villains together only slightly surpassed the heroines, and did not equal the wetness of the heroes. Generally speaking, one can safely conclude that the commercial movies are dripping wet.

To the Dale studies which established the central trends of the commercial movies of 1920 to 1932 may be added the analyses of 142 pictures made by Peters and his associates. They conducted in their study of movies and mores [12] four

---

[12] *Motion Pictures and Standards of Morality*, by Charles C. Peters.

interesting analyses of details of pictures which appeared in the local theaters. In 142 pictures they found 726 scenes depicting aggressiveness of girls in love-making; of these actions 549 were performed by attractive characters and 177 by unattractive persons. They found also in the 142 pictures, 741 scenes of kissing and caressing mostly by casual lovers (383); partly by betrothed lovers (200), and partly by married persons (157). They analyzed the 142 pictures for democractic attitudes and practices and found 303 scenes depicting the treatment of employees and subordinates, 250 scenes in which social "superiors" dealt with social "inferiors," and 60 scenes in which racial discrimination was present. In the same pictures they observed and rated 522 scenes depicting the treatment of children by parents— 97 involving the discipline of children, 347 involving companionship with children, and 78 depicting self-sacrifice of parents for children. The quality of these scenes will be described later.

Movies and Conduct and *Movies, Delinquency, and Crime* present by implication an additional mass of information about the content of commercial pictures. One can deduce the content of pictures by watching the play of children and noting their phantasy life. Dress and manners of the characters are noted and imitated. Techniques of love-making are found and copied. Fear pictures, sentimental pictures, and exciting films abound and exert their influence. Strivings for ambitious ends are presented and arouse ambitions in a variety of directions. The freedom of youth and the adventurous lives of the characters are represented and may cause discontent with homes and neighborhoods to arise. Some plays portray family affection and loyalty and to these many children respond successfully.

Crime pictures have a pronounced effect upon delinquents. Minor delinquencies are aggravated by these pictures in many cases; cues for criminal actions are presented and are sometimes copied by young delinquents. The "easy money" and the luxury shown in the movies leave traces in the memories and conduct of delinquents. Criminal-action pictures make some youths "want to fight" because of emotional possession. "You get a lot of thrill out of them." Crime pictures aggravate daydreaming about lives of crime. Techniques of crime are numerous in pictures and concretely portrayed. Blumer and Hauser collected from their materials a large number of techniques that had been noted and sometimes used by delinquents: how to open a safe by the feel of the dial, how to act and what to do in robbery with a gun, how to jimmy a window, how to force an automobile door with a piece of pipe, how to take doors off hinges in burglarizing a house, eluding police in the dark, how to pick pockets, the use of ether in burglarizing, putting burglar alarms out of commission, and so on and so on. To be sure, the delinquent might have learned these techniques without the movies. We had delinquency before commercial motion pictures were invented. But crime movies are handy and it is easy to learn from them if one is interested in delinquent behavior. One's education in crime advances more rapidly by means of crime pictures.

The sex pictures have an extremely powerful influence upon many delinquents. Sexual passions are aroused and amateur prostitution is aggravated. The fast life depicted by the movie characters on the screen induces desires, they say, for such a life. Luxury and smart appearance make an enormous appeal, particularly to many female delinquents. Granted that reports from delinquents are not completely reliable, the fact still remains that enough of them can quote chapter and verse to show that crime and sex pictures are at least an aggravating influence in their conduct.

From all these data collected about the content of pictures the conclusion is inevitable that from the point of view of children's welfare the commercial movies are an unsavory mess. For adults the selection of movies is their own business, to be controlled by whatever means they want to use. But children have crashed the gate in millions—eager-minded, ripe for learning; and three weeks out of four on their once-a-week trips to the movies they see a crime picture, a love picture, and a sex picture. The producers ought to have a heart.

Peters [13] devised a technique for judging whether pictures were morally "good" or "bad." The technique perfected was quite ingenious. He assumes that pictures are good if they are congruent with the mores, beliefs, or conventions and are bad if they are in conflict with them. This means that goodness or badness is based upon the sensibilities of the people concerned. These sensibilities by which groups come to feel that certain acts are "bad" and others "good" are the product of long experience and are more than likely to be correct for their time and place. These group feelings come to be accepted by the individuals who make up the group, so that one can get evidence of the attitude of the group as a whole from the reaction of a comparatively few of its members. In this sense, then, the "morality" of motion pictures may be gauged by securing the response of a comparatively small number of "judges" who because they have assimilated the point of view of their group, can speak for the group. But in most communities there are several groups and consequently

[13] *Motion Pictures and Standards of Morality*, by Charles C. Peters.

several "public opinions" about moral questions, so that parents, for instance, who seek for good pictures for their children must either see them themselves or trust the judgment of some person or group whose tastes and beliefs they believe to be like their own.

Relying upon this definition of morality Peters proceeded to study four types of scenes in pictures: aggressiveness of a girl in love-making, kissing and caressing, democratic attitudes and practices, and the treatment of children by parents.

The method used was the same in each case. He first constructed a scale of incidents in each area. This was done by collecting a large number of incidents related to each— and then asking each of several groups of persons to rate the incidents as "admired," disapproved, or neutral. Upon this basis by the use of statistical procedures he was able to rank the incidents from the extremes of approval to the opposite extreme of disapproval. In carrying out the procedure he was able to secure quantities to express the attitude of such groups as college professors, young miners, ministers, factory girls, "society girls," and the like. Incidentally, the college professors and their wives were the most conservative of all the groups on the issues studied. In the scale for aggressive love-making the order of the groups ranked from conservativeness to liberality were: faculty, adult Brethren, preachers of the United States, college senior boys, college senior girls, young Brethren, Junior League girls, Hampton Institute Negroes, graduate students, members of the Motion Picture Research Council, business men, factory workers, adult miners, and young miners. The position of the Research Council members among the least conservative groups is of passing interest.

When the scales were perfected five observers were

trained to analyze each of 142 pictures in the theater and to place the scenes in their appropriate places on the scale. The composite judgment of the five observers was calculated for each scene and the positions of the scenes were compared with the judgments of the groups whose positions upon the scales had been determined as indicated.

In the 142 pictures 522 scenes depicting the treatment of children by parents were observed. Of these 445 were scenes in which the parents were attractive characters and 77 were unattractive. In these scenes the conduct of parents in the movies was above the average of the groups from the standpoint of whose moral codes the scales were made. If one sets the approval of the upper 25 per cent of each group as a high standard of excellence, 41 per cent of the scenes were satisfactory. Seventy per cent of all the scenes were satisfactory to the average of the groups. Thus on the whole the treatment of children tends in an upward rather than a downward direction. On the average children are treated better in the movies than they are treated outside.

In the 142 pictures 741 kissing and caressing scenes were studied. Of these Peters says "the conduct in motion pictures, as far as kissing is concerned, is closely parallel to that of life in the six social groups studied so far as the conduct of attractive characters is concerned but the conduct in motion pictures is worse than life when we consider both attractive and unattractive characters."

In the study of democratic attitudes 303 scenes were observed in which the treatment of employees, "inferior" races, and persons of "inferior" social standing were rated. Here "the findings indicate that motion pictures stand rather above the mores in respect to democratic attitudes and practices."

In aggressiveness of a girl in love-making the case is less

favorable. In 726 scenes studied, of which 549 were played by attractive characters, it was found that only 12 per cent of the scenes were such as half the combined groups would admire and 56 per cent of the scenes would be actively disapproved by half the groups. Eighty-five per cent would be disapproved by the upper quarter of the groups. Among the groups 95 per cent of the scenes would be disapproved by the upper 25 per cent of strict adult Brethren; but 64 per cent were disapproved even by the upper quarter of adolescent miners—the most liberal. And 25 per cent of the scenes would be disapproved by three quarters of the young miners. When Peters studied the relation of practice in this area with approved standards he found that practice was also below the approved level and that motion-picture conduct in aggressiveness of girls was about on a level with practice. "It is clear," writes Peters, "that motion pictures are bucking hard against present standards of value in relation to aggressiveness in love-making. Practice, too, seems to be taking the reins but against a certain feeling of propriety yet persisting. It is clear that the mores (in the sense of *approved* customs) cannot long lag behind practice; especially when the suggestions of skillfully constructed drama tend constantly to give sanction to the deviating patterns and thus win approval for them."

The major points of interest in this study are two in number. First Peters has clearly defined good and bad. They are determined by the approval of judges. A picture is good if congruent with the mores and bad if in conflict with them. This holds for the mores of individuals or of groups. And as has been remarked above, the practical procedures for a parent in selecting pictures for children to see if he cannot pre-view them himself is to take the opinion of individuals or groups whose taste he believes to be like his own. Second, some scenes in the movies are admired, others merit disapproval of all Peters' groups. But in the matter of aggressive love-making by girls the conduct depicted in the movies is distinctly below the approved standards of every group studied.

TEACHING DISCRIMINATION TO CHILDREN

IN conclusion the investigators attacked the control of motion-picture influence in one direction. They concluded that they could experiment with one constructive safeguard against bad movies and one aid to good movies. Dale [14] accordingly prepared a textbook for high-school boys and girls on motion-picture appreciation and criticism. The intent was to teach the adolescent how to judge pictures for himself by setting standards, and to teach him how to apply them. It was believed that a discriminating audience would be a constructive power for control of what would be produced.

The techniques of assembling the materials were simple because motion pictures are a form of art and drama. In these fields the underlying principles have already been worked out and used in the high-school study of art appreciation and literature including the drama. These were assembled from authoritative sources and applied to the photoplay. In making the applications the assistance of experts in the appropriate fields was secured. When the materials were assembled they were tried out experimentally in selected schools in 1931 to 1932. During 1932 to 1933 the materials are being revised again in connection with the teaching of motion-picture appreciation over the radio broadcast to high-school students and adult discussion groups. It is also being used on a wider scale in high schools

[14] *How to Appreciate Motion Pictures*, by Edgar Dale.

than in the previous year. Particularly fruitful contacts were made with the Photoplay Committee of the National Council of Teachers of English. This contact is valuable because the normal avenue of approach to the teaching of motion-picture appreciation in the high school is through teachers of courses in English and because the Committee of the Council has been vigorously promoting motion-picture appreciation for two or three years. The experimental program of the committee is meeting with success in utilizing the unusual interest of high-school students in motion pictures, and promises to be a constructive measure in teaching adolescents how to discriminate among motion pictures—to help them to enjoy good art and drama more deeply and criticize bad pictures more intelligently.

CONCLUSION

As one reviews the series of studies three conclusions seem inevitable. First, the motion picture, as such, is a potent medium of education. Children even of the early age of 8 see half the facts in a picture and remember them for a surprisingly long time. A single exposure to a picture may produce a measurable change in attitude. Emotions are measurably stirred as the scenes of a drama unfold and this excitement may be recorded in deviations from the norm in sleep patterns, by visible gross evidences of bodily movement and by refined internal responses. They constitute patterns of conduct in daydreaming, phantasy, and action. The evidence of their influence is massive and irrefutable.

Second, for children the content of current pictures is not good. There is too much sex and crime and love for a balanced diet for children. These impartial studies reveal much more harm than help. Stoddard, Thurstone, Ruckmick, Blumer, and their associates indicate the power of the motion picture. But Dale, Blumer, Thrasher, Peters, and their associates clearly indicate that the power flows too much in dangerous directions.

Third, the motion-picture situation is very complicated. It is one among many influences which mold the experience of children. How powerful this is in relation to the influence of the ideals taught in the home, in the school, and in the church by street life and companions or by community customs, these studies have not canvassed. May and Shuttleworth found in their survey study that in attitude toward the great majority of specific objects examined there was little difference between those children who go often to the movies and those who attend infrequently. That the more exactly controlled studies of Stoddard, Thurstone, and others showed specific and significant differences produced, complicates the question of total influence. The situation is further complicated by the fact that the producers and exhibitors have not separated the child problem from the adult problem. That is to say, they show pictures indiscriminately, to an audience consisting of minors and adults in the proportion of one minor to two adults. This causes a serious difficulty in this respect. Pictures may theoretically be satisfactory for adults and harmful to children. Presumably a much wider range of subjects and even more liberal standard for morality may be presented to adults than to children. Theoretically an adult is a free agent, but children need protection.

If, then, all pictures are constructed with only the welfare of children in mind, complications arise because adults may not be satisfied with them for themselves. Whether they should be satisfied with pictures good for children is of course a question which arouses heated controversy.

But whatever the answer, it still remains that the producers and exhibitors provide pictures for the public in general and with few exceptions they offer them as though the audiences consisted entirely of adults.

Exclusion of children from all theaters is clearly not the solution. It cannot be done because the children would crash the gate to see the thrilling scenes. Nothing of equal interest to children has happened in the world of drama before. In books, the adult drama cannot be understood by the children. In the theaters they cannot comprehend the legitimate drama. But the movie is within their comprehension and they clamor to attend.

It is inevitable, therefore, that producers of motion pictures who have a love for children and an interest in their development must address themselves to the problems of children's movies as the publishers of books have attacked the problems of providing a children's literature. Here again many problems emerge, but ingenuity will be equal to them because the welfare of children is so important. In the field of literature, scores of publishing houses produce children's books exclusively. In the field of motion pictures there undoubtedly is a place for similar institutions which would produce simply constructed pictures for children and show them in simply equipped theaters, or on special days at theaters for adults. All educators know that children's tastes are very simple; ornate pictures produced with high-salaried stars are not necessary. Theaters for children need only to be safe, sanitary, and comfortable. The experience of publishers indicates the probable success of such ventures. But whatever the solution it is evident that the producer has a direct responsibility in solving this problem.

The responsibility of course does not rest solely with the

producers, although it rests primarily with them: children now have to take what is offered to them. But parents in the presence of what we find in the theaters must exercise great care to see that their children are encouraged to see good pictures and are defended from bad ones.

The solutions of the movie problem have not been studied in these fact-finding investigations. There is no single solution nor formula that will meet the situation. The best procedure is to find the facts and publish them to stimulate discussion from which programs of action will eventually crystallize.

Certainly the problem of the movies and the children is so important and critical that parents, producers, and public must willingly and intelligently coöperate to reach some happy solution. The producers occupy the key position. The public at present must take, within the limits of the censorship of the states, whatever pictures are made.

The situation points unmistakably to the establishment by the producers of a children's department whose primary function will be to experiment, to invent, to try out, to eliminate, to press persistently until they produce proper solutions to the problem. This research organization is clearly indicated. It does not appear that such experimentation would be expensive. The simple obligation rests upon those producers who love children to find a way of making the motion picture a beautiful, fascinating, and kindly servant of childhood.

INDEX

Adult discount, 42f.
Appreciation and criticism of movies by children, 59
Attendance at movies, 5, 44ff.
Attitudes, of movie fans, 14ff.; cumulative effect upon, 21ff.; effect of one exposure upon, 20; influence of movies upon, 5, 11; measures of, 18ff.; permanence of effect upon, 23ff.
Authority of movies in child life, 9, 40f.

Blumer, Herbert, 2, 3, 4, 10, 13, 16, 23, 24, 29, 31, 36, 37, 40, 41, 42, 43, 47, 51, 61

Conclusions, 60ff.
Conduct, influence of movies upon 5, 35ff.; of movie fans, 12ff.
Conflict of movies with mores, 55ff.; aggressiveness of girls in love-making, 53f., 57f.; democratic attitudes, 57; kissing and caressing, 57; treatment of children, 57
Content of current movies, 5, 47ff.; effects of upon delinquents, 54f.; goals of characters in, 52f.; liquor in, 52f.; love, sex, and crime in, 49ff.; sex details in, 51f.; types of criminal in, 49f.; weapons in, 50f.
Cressey, Paul G., 2, 3, 12, 13, 36

Dale, Edgar, 3, 43, 44, 47, 48, 50, 52, 59, 61
Dysinger, W. S., 3, 9, 25, 27, 28, 31

Emotional detachment, 42f.
Emotional possession, 38ff.
Emotions, influence of movies upon, 5, 25, 29; danger, conflict or tragedy, 26; erotic scenes, 26ff.

Good pictures, definition of, 58

Hauser, Philip M., 2, 3, 36
Health, influence of movies upon, 5, 31
Holaday, P. W., 7, 10, 11, 27, 31, 40

Individual differences, 27, 34f.
Information, amount remembered, 8; how long remembered, 8; influence of movies upon, 5, 7ff.; what is best remembered, 10ff.
Initiation of the studies, 1

Limitations of movie influence, 17ff., 61

Marquis, Dorothy P., 3, 31
May, Mark A., 2, 4, 11, 14, 16, 17, 61
Miller, Vernon L., 3, 31
Motion Picture Research Council, 1, 2, 3, 4, 7, 56
Movies referred to: *Alibi*, 20, 21; *All Quiet on the Western Front*, 20, 21, 22, 23; *Big House*, 20, 21, 22; *Charlie Chan's Chance*, 26; *Fighting Caravans*, 7; *Four Sons*, 20, 21; *Hide Out*, 20, 21; *His Woman*, 26; *Hop to it, Bell Hop*, 25; *Journey's End*, 20, 21, 22; *New Moon*, 7; *Numbered Men*, 20, 21, 22; *Passion Flower*, 7; *Rango*, 7; *Son of the Gods*, 20, 23, 24; *Stolen Heaven*, 7; *Street of Chance*, 20, 21; *The Birth of a Nation*, 20, 21; *The Criminal Code*, 20, 21, 22; *The Feast of Ishtar*, 26, 27; *The Iron Mule*, 26; *The Road to Singapore*, 26; *The Valiant*, 20, 21; *The Yellow Ticket*, 26; *Tom Sawyer*, 7, 9; *Welcome Danger*, 20, 21

Peters, Charles C., 47, 51, 52, 55, 56, 57, 58, 59, 61
Peterson, Ruth C., 2, 11, 17, 18, 23, 31, 40
Plan of the studies, 4ff.

65

Renshaw, Samuel, 3, 17, 31
Responsibilities of the producers, 60ff.
Ruckmick, Christian A., 3, 9, 17, 25, 27, 28, 31, 42, 51, 60

Sex differences, 11, 28
Shuttleworth, Frank K., 2, 11, 14, 16, 17, 61
Sleep, decrease in motility in, 34; increase in motility in, 33f.; influence of movies upon, 31ff.; normal sleep patterns, 32f.
Stoddard, George D., 7, 10, 11, 16, 27, 31, 40, 60, 61

Thrasher, Frederick M., 2, 3, 4, 10, 12, 13, 16, 36, 41, 47, 61
Thurstone, L. L., 2, 11, 16, 17, 18, 23, 31, 40, 60, 61